A Place to Take Your Shame

A Place to Take Your Shame

God is calling His daughters to Rise up from the Ashes of their Pain and be Restored to their Place in His Palace.

Misty Price

XULON PRESS

Xulon Press
2301 Lucien Way #415
Maitland, FL 32751
407.339.4217
www.xulonpress.com

© 2019 by Misty Price

All rights reserved solely by the author. The author guarantees all contents are original and do not infringe upon the legal rights of any other person or work. No part of this book may be reproduced in any form without the permission of the author. The views expressed in this book are not necessarily those of the publisher.

Unless otherwise indicated, Scripture quotations taken from the New King James Version (NKJV). Copyright © 1982 by Thomas Nelson, Inc. Used by permission. All rights reserved.

Printed in the United States of America.

ISBN-13: 978-1-5456-7989-0

Dedication Page

I dedicate this book to a close friend of mine who shall remain anonymous. When we were in elementary school, she disobeyed her mother and snuck out of her house for the evening, only to be violently gang raped. She was too afraid to tell her mother what had happened because she had disobeyed when she snuck out of the house. I wanted so desperately to be able to say something that would make her pain stop. I myself was quietly suffering from the pain of being sexually abused as a small child.

This book is dedicated to victims everywhere and those who want to minister to them.

Thank you to my husband, Phillip, for your support. I love you. Thank you to my favorite daughter, Sabrina, and my favorite son, Caleb. I love you both.

Contents

Introduction ix

Chapter One The First Evil 1

Chapter Two The Second Evil is Worse 15

Chapter Three A Father's Response 27

Chapter Four Choose to Forgive 37

Chapter Five Grieve the Loss & Break the Cycle 47

Chapter Six Jesus's Blood Cleanses Me 61

Chapter Seven Starting New 67

Answer Key 69

About the Author 77

End Notes 79

INTRODUCTION

God is restoring His daughters to their rightful position of power in His kingdom! God never intended for His daughters to be held back, mistreated, or abused. Perhaps you, a family member, or a friend have experienced this pain, or maybe as a minister, you encounter those who have. If so, this workbook is for you. This workbook will walk you through seven chapters based on seven biblical principles that if applied to your life will help you overcome the devastation of abuse. As a victim myself, I have experienced relief and victory through the process clearly outlined in this workbook. As a minister, I have shared this process with several girls and women in the last twenty-five years and have seen them experience freedom as well. God desires to give you beauty for your ashes. Choose to rise up from the pain and allow Him to restore you.

Chapter One

THE FIRST EVIL

2 Samuel 13:1-14 (NKJV)

1 After this Absalom the son of David had a lovely sister, whose name was Tamar; and Amnon the son of David loved her. 2 Amnon was so distressed over his sister Tamar that he became sick; for she was a virgin. And it was improper for Amnon to do anything to her.
3 But Amnon had a friend whose name was Jonadab the son of Shimeah, David's brother. Now Jonadab was a very crafty man. 4 And he said to him, "Why are you, the king's son, becoming thinner day after day? Will you not tell me?" Amnon said to him, "I love Tamar, my brother Absalom's sister."
5 So Jonadab said to him, "Lie down on your bed and pretend to be ill. And when your father comes to see you, say to him, 'Please let my sister Tamar come and give me food, and prepare the food in my sight, that I may see it and eat it from her hand.'"
6 Then Amnon lay down and pretended to be ill; and when the king came to see him, Amnon said to the king, 'Please let Tamar my sister come and make a couple of cakes for me in my sight, that I may eat from her hand.'"
7 And David sent home to Tamar, saying, "Now go to your brother Amnon's house, and prepare food for him." 8 So Tamar went to her brother Amnon's house; and he was lying down. Then she took flour

and kneaded it, made cakes in his sight, and baked the cakes. **9** *And she took the pan and placed them out before him, but he refused to eat. Then Amnon said, "Have everyone go out from me." And they all went out from him.*

10 *Then Amnon said to Tamar, "Bring the food into the bedroom, that I may eat from your hand." And Tamar took the cakes which she had made, and brought them to Amnon her brother in the bedroom.* **11** *Now when she had brought them to him to eat, he took hold of her and said to her, "Come, lie with me, my sister."*

12 *But she answered him. "No, my brother, do not force me, for no such thing should be done in Israel. <u>Do not do this disgraceful thing!</u>* **13** *"<u>And I, where could I take my shame</u>? And as for you, you would be like one of the fools in Israel. Now therefore, please speak to the king; for he will not withhold me from you."*

14 *However, he would not heed her voice; and being stronger than she, he forced her and lay with her.*

Being a Woman in Old Testament Bible Times

In the Old Testament, the religious customs and traditions and social laws in the Jewish community mandated that women could not work or own land. They were dependent on the men in their lives to provide financially for them. This started with their fathers, who provided for them until he chose a spouse for them. In today's time period, it may seem cruel and unfair for a father to select his daughter's husband. However, this was done with the intent to hold women in high regard—to protect them and care for them. The father would choose a groom that would be able to provide for his daughter in a similar or better manner than he did, and the father was most familiar with his daughter's personality, expectations, skills, limits, belief system, emotional needs, and comfort level. The groom was required to give the father of the bride a dowry, which was proof of the groom's ability to provide financial stability for the daughter.

Although this system was practiced to ensure provision for women, there are always going to be some people in life who choose to take advantage of a system for their own gain. Unfortunately, we see an example of a father giving his daughter in marriage for his own benefit and not hers in Genesis 31:15. In Old Testament times, it also seemed common for kings to give their daughters to marry princes of other nations, thus ensuring peace between the two nations with the marrying of the children (1 Kings 3:1) Although these marriages were for political reasons, it kept with the tradition of a young girl being provided for in a similar financial lifestyle. The father was also obligated to ensure that his daughter was a virgin upon giving her in marriage. In fact, it was against the law and punishable by death for a father to give his daughter in marriage if she was not a virgin. Deuteronomy 22:17 records in detail how a father is to respond if the accusation of giving his non-virgin daughter in marriage is made against him.

Tamar's Father

The first two verses of 2 Samuel 13 explain the family relation between Amnon and Tamar. During this time period, it was acceptable to have more than one wife, so David was the father to both Amnon and Tamar. Amnon and Tamar were half-brother and sister, while Absalom and Tamar had the same mother and father.

Unless you are new to the Bible, you likely are familiar with who David was. David was rejected by his own father and left to tend sheep, which at the time was considered a lowly job, while his brothers were thought of more highly in the eyes of their father. But David was chosen by God and anointed by the prophet Samuel to be the next king over the nation of Israel, God's chosen people. It was said by God in 1 Samuel 13:14 that David was a man after "his own heart." Before actually being crowned king, David was the boy with the slingshot that took down the giant that opposed and taunted God's people. Before becoming king, David was a mighty warrior that God used to bring His people out of the oppression of the Philistines. He was a type of Christ, an Old Testament deliverer. He was also a worshipper and poured his heart out to God, and it was under the anointing of his music that the distressing spirit lifted off of Saul (1 Sam. 16:23). When David became king, he had a vision to unite the fragmented nation of God's people, the houses of Judah and Israel, and restore temple worship. David was arguably the greatest Old Testament king of Israel.

Prior to 2 Samuel 13, in 2 Samuel 11, we see that David fell into sexual sin and orchestrated murder to cover it up. As a result, God sent the prophet Nathan to confront David. The consequences of his actions were that the child conceived during David's sin would die and that the sword would not depart from David's home (2 Sam. 12:10-14). David repented and remained king, and his kingship remained strong, even during the events of 2 Samuel 11-13.

Life as a Princess

Let's think about what life must have been like for Tamar prior to the event of her half-brother forcing himself on her sexually. Tamar and Absalom were the children of Maacah. In 2 Samuel 3:3, it tells us that Maacah was the daughter of Talmai, who was the king of Geshur. This means that Tamar had royalty in her blood from both her mother and father. Tamar would have been used to a luxurious lifestyle. She was destined to likely be married to a prince or someone who for sure could continue to provide the lifestyle she had grown accustomed to in her father's palace. It is likely that she had her own quarters and/or servants in the palace. She would have been accustomed to wearing and having nice, expensive things.

Today, our society is captivated by socialites, celebrities, and heiresses that are wealthy or in line to inherit great wealth. The media follows them around to get pictures of their lavish lifestyle or out-of-control spending habits. Tamar was a real princess, and the wealth she had access to would probably make the heiresses of today look poor. Her husband would have been expected to provide for her in a similar way.

As the king's virgin daughter, she wore a beautiful robe that was given to her by her father, King David. The robe, coat, or garment of that day was a symbol of somebody's status in society. It told about a person and the family that he or she belonged to. In today's society, perhaps it could be compared to the type of wedding ring one wears. If you wear a wedding ring, you know it is symbolic of your commitment or wedding vow to another person. The size of the diamond on your ring might show the wealth or status that your spouse is able to provide for you. King David gave all his virgin daughters such a robe. We can safely speculate that the robe was very elegant and costly. Any young women living in that time period would probably have loved to have worn such a thing. King David was certainly proud of his virgin daughters, and the robe symbolized his love, care, and protection toward them, as well as their royal position in the nation of Israel. Since the Bible says King David gave these robes to his virgin daughters, the robes also symbolized their virginity and purity (2 Sam. 13:18). The robe draped on her beautiful body would have commanded respect. Everybody that viewed the robe would know she was not a common person but royalty. Tamar probably felt special every time she put it on. In addition to being born into the right family, she was also born a naturally beautiful young woman. Still, as we know, abuse, pain, death, sickness, and suffering know no socioeconomic boundary or prejudice.

Abuse and Power

The Merriam-Webster dictionary defines the word abuse, when used as a verb, as "to put to a wrong or improper use and to use or treat so as to injure or damage." Abuse happens when a person exerts power over an unwilling person, a victim. Power can be exerted in many different forms. A person can have physical strength over another person. A person can also have power in the form of authority or influence, such as a teacher over a student, a boss over an employee, a pastor over a parishioner, or a government official over a citizen. As defined by each state, there are statutory rape laws that acknowledge an adult has power over a child that is below the age of consent. When a person chooses to use or exert his or her power over another individual for wrong, improper use, or damage, this is abuse. There are many forms of abuse, such as physical, sexual, and verbal, just to name a few. Sometimes abusers will go to great lengths to groom or stalk an individual until they have lured them into a place where they can exert power over them in the form of abuse. If you are the survivor of any kind of abuse, whether one time or multiple times during the course of several years, you can apply your situation through this workbook every time you see the phrase "your hurt."

There is nothing in Scripture that would lead us to believe that Tamar did anything wrong on her part to instigate these events. There is no biblical evidence to prove that Tamar had sinned or suggests that anything she had previously done brought these circumstances upon herself. At the time of this horrible event, she was simply obeying her father to visit her sick brother and care for him in a very practical way by baking food for him. We see what Tamar couldn't in the previous verses, that Amnon was setting a trap for her to get her alone so he could exert his power over her for his own selfish gratification. The text says that Amnon loved Tamar; however, his actions are contrary to what the Bible defines as love. First Corinthians 13:4-5 says, "Love suffers long and is kind; love does not envy; love does not parade itself, is not puffed up; does not behave rudely, does not seek its own, is not provoked, thinks no evil." Amnon's actions toward Tamar did not demonstrate love that puts the other person first. Instead his love was very selfish and seeking its own, even to the point of causing great harm toward Tamar.

Is it my Fault?

Tamar was horrified by her half-brother's suggestion, "Come lie with me." She quickly realized that she was at his mercy and begged him not to rape her. She was able to see that his mind had been made up, however, and that he would not be satisfied until he was with her sexually. So, she committed to marry him if he would simply ask her father first. This was the custom and the proper thing to do. Deep down inside, this may not have been the man that she truly wanted to marry; however, it would be better than the alternative that the rape would leave her to bear. She was able to think ahead and perceive the outcome of what Amnon wanted to do to her. She understood the shame that would be brought on her for the rest of her life, and she spoke to him of how he would be seen as a fool. Still, even after her pleas, cries for mercy, and attempts to reason with him, it was futile. He did what he wanted with no regard for her or the consequences. He used her for his own physical pleasure—forcing her, humiliating her, and disregarding her. Since she was not willing, his treatment of her was rough, ugly, cruel, and harsh. At this point, there was nothing Tamar could have done to keep this situation from happening—no clever words, nothing.

Similar to Tamar's situation, your abuser may have been setting a trap for you all along. Sometimes victims may unknowingly put themselves in a vulnerable or unwise situation due to poor choices or simply being naive. If a young girl does not understand the value of her God-given virginity, she may unknowingly put herself in vulnerable or compromising situations. This makes the case for all young people to receive good biblical training on the purpose God has for giving them the gift of virginity. Young girls especially need to learn how to guard and protect this gift. Still, nobody deserves to be abused.

A woman does not cause a man to commit such acts against her; it is the issue of his own heart that causes him to choose to abuse. Do not carry the burden of somebody else's sin. Scripture is clear that victims of rape should not be "victim shamed." The victim is not to be blamed, according to Deuteronomy 22:25-27:

But if a man finds a betrothed young woman in the countryside, and the man forces her and lies with her, then only the man who lay with her shall die. But you shall do nothing to the young woman; there is in the young woman no sin deserving of death, for just as when a man rises against his neighbor and kills him, even so is this matter. For he found her in the countryside, and the betrothed young woman cried out, but there was no one to save her.

A Modern-Day Tamar

There was a young girl named Tammy who was a senior in high school. She was an honor roll student and enjoyed cheer and dance. She was looking forward to going to college to study elementary education so she could work with small children. Her parents were caring and hard-working, always wanting what was best for her. Her senior year of high school, she planned to go to the prom with her longtime friend Jake. However, her parents weren't too fond of Jake because he came from an unstable home. It was not likely that Jake would be able to afford to go away to college. Tammy's father worked with a gentleman whose son, Bryan, was a senior too and had already received a full scholarship to the state university.

Tammy's father insisted that she go to prom with Bryan, who had always seemed to show an interest in Tammy. This was not really what Tammy wanted, but she wanted to please her parents, so she agreed to go with him. What she didn't know was that Bryan had an older friend already at the state university who had convinced Bryan that if he wanted to be accepted into their group when he started college in the fall, he needed to show up with proof that he had had sex on his prom night. This was kind of a rite of passage or initiation to be accepted into the group. This friend had also given Bryan a few ideas about how he could do this, even encouraging Bryan to go to his local pharmacy and buy cough medicine to slip into his prom date's drink if she was unwilling to cooperate.

Bryan was a perfect gentleman the night he picked Tammy up from her parents' house. He showed up with a corsage, he opened the door for her as she stepped into his truck, and they enjoyed a meal at a fancy restaurant before arriving at the prom. Bryan had even agreed to have Tammy home by 1:30 am. Prom was dismissed at midnight, and he told Tammy that he had promised the guys on his basketball team that he would at least make an appearance at their party. Tammy was reluctant, but Bryan promised they wouldn't stay long and was certain that some of her friends would be there also.

Upon arriving at the house, Tammy quickly noticed that everybody was cramped into a small, living-room area and there were no adults at the party. The home smelled horribly of smoke that immediately made her dizzy. Bryan quickly joined his friends in the kitchen drinking beer; it seemed all too natural for him. Apparently, this wasn't the first drinking party he had been to. The smoke and loud music didn't seem to bother him a bit. Tammy leaned up against a wall by the kitchen door. She did not want to join the others in the kitchen drinking, but she couldn't handle all the smoke in the living room. One of Bryan's friends walked out of the kitchen and handed Tammy a cold can of soda that had already been opened. "Lighten up; Bryan will be ready to leave soon," he said. She began sipping the soda and noticed there was a bathroom down the hallway in front of her. She walked into the bathroom and closed the door behind her. She thought it was nice and quiet in there. She started to feel dizzy and could see the room was starting to spin. She heard someone banging on the bathroom door. Everything after that seemed like a blur. The next thing she could remember was being naked on a bed, crying and begging Bryan to stop touching her. She also seemed to remember a light going off or flashing in her face like maybe someone was taking pictures.

A Place to Take Your Shame

Questions Chapter One

After reading each chapter, you will see questions that pertain specifically to the chapter. Do your best to answer them in detail. If additional space is needed, I encourage you to purchase a journal to complete your answers. There is an answer key included at the end of the book.

Growing up in O.T. Bible times:
1. Were women allowed to work or own property?

_____

_____

_____

2. How were women provided for financially?

_____

_____

_____

3. How did a father choose a groom for his daughter?

_____

_____

_____

4. What happened if a man gave his daughter in marriage and she was found not to be a virgin?

_____

_____

_____

THE FIRST EVIL

About Tamar:

5. Who was Tamar's father?

_____

6. Who was Tamar's mother?

_____

7. How was Amnon related to Tamar?

_____

8. How was Absalom related to Tamar?

_____

9. Describe Tamar's lifestyle?

_____

_____

_____

10. As a princess of two countries, what should Tamar's future have looked like?

_____

_____

_____

11. What did the robe that Tamar wore symbolize?

_____

_____

_____

A Place to Take Your Shame

12. Why did Tamar go to Amnon's house, and who told her to go?

_____
_____
_____

13. What did Tamar do to try to stop Amnon from forcing her?

_____
_____
_____

14. Did Tamar deserve to be raped?

_____
_____
_____

About you:

15. According to Deuteronomy 22:25-27, is "victim shaming" a biblical response that God approves of?

_____
_____
_____

16. Did you deserve to be raped, abused, or misused?

_____
_____
_____

17. In Tamar's situation, Amnon exerted physical power over Tamar. Is physical force a requirement for abuse to take place?

_____

_____

_____

Closing Prayer: Lord, please help me as I begin this journey of healing and restoration.

Chapter Two

THE SECOND EVIL IS WORSE

2 Samuel 13:15-20 (NKJV)
15 Then Amnon hated her exceedingly, so that the hatred with which he hated her was greater than the love with which he had loved her. And Amnon said to her, "Arise, be gone!"
16 <u>So she said to him, "No, indeed! This evil of sending me away is worse than the other that you did to me."</u> But he would not listen to her.
17 Then he called his servant who attended him, and said, "Here! Put this woman out, away from me, and bolt the door behind her."
18 Now she had on a robe of many colors, for the king's virgin daughters wore such apparel. And his servant put her out and bolted the door behind her. 19 Then Tamar put ashes on her head, and tore her robe of many colors that was on her, and laid her hand on her head and went away crying bitterly.
20 And Absalom her brother said to her, "Has Amnon your brother been with you? But now hold your peace, my sister. He is your brother; do not take this thing to heart." So Tamar remained desolate in her brother Absalom's house.

The Second Evil is Worse
  Amnon was not displaying true biblical love for Tamar. Now, those feelings of love he had once carried had turned to hate. Amnon

demanded that Tamar be gone from his presence. She pleaded with him, but he showed no mercy or compassion toward her. The only feeling he now had for her was hate. Amnon called for one of his servants, whom he had previously asked to leave the room, to come back into the room. He instructed the servant to take Tamar not only from his room but out of the house. Tamar was used to being treated with respect and was now treated as a commoner, an enemy, and it seems that the servant likely laid hands on her, physically forcing her out the door.

Before Tamar was raped, she was referred to in 2 Samuel 13:1, as "lovely." After Amnon raped Tamar, he now referred to her as "that woman." He dehumanized her and attached disgust and shame to her name that was not there before. Amnon's new-found hate for Tamar was not her fault. This was a result of the issues in his own heart. However, he sentenced her to a life of silent shame alone after bolting the door behind her. She was now forced to bear the consequences of his sin.

Sentenced to a Life of Shame

What did Tamar mean by saying that this second evil was worse than the first? Obviously, the first evil was the act of being raped. I suspect that she meant the second evil was the evil of being rejected and put out of the house because it was this action that would force Tamar to live as an outcast of society and even as a reject from her own family. In many cases, the physical effects of rape will heal; the physical wounds on the body will recover. However, it is the emotional pain or trauma of being forced, rejected, or cast out that is far more difficult to recover and heal from. Tamar put ashes on her head, which in her day was an outward sign showing that she was in a state of great grieving. She tore the beautiful robe that her father had given her—no longer was she fit to wear it. No longer could she parade herself around town as one of King David's lovely, beautiful virgin daughters. She now had to hide in shame. No longer was she worthy to be given in marriage. She could not look forward to the day when she would marry a handsome young man that would provide for her. No longer could she look forward to fulfilling her duties of having and raising children. Her life was changed the moment Amnon forced himself on her. Without a husband or the ability to work, what would life look like for Tamar now? What kind of life would she be sentenced to live?

A State of Desolation

Tamar remained a desolate woman in her brother Absalom's house. The Merriam-Webster dictionary defines "desolate" as "devoid of inhabitants, comfort or hope; joyless, sorrowful, and showing the effects of abandonment and neglect." In Tamar's time period, there was not a plan or provision for her situation. Society had not yet prepared for such situations. As a result, sadly, Tamar did remain without hope in a state of desolation. For the purpose of this workbook, let's define the phrase "state of desolation" as without hope or comfort—a frame of mind, a false self-perception, or way of thinking after the first evil or hurt that happened.

Today in our society, women are allowed to be given in marriage, even if they are not virgins. They are allowed to work, own property, and marry freely as they choose. However, there are many women today that still remain in a silent state of desolation. Our circumstances may look fine on the outside, just like our physical bodies may have healed and look whole. But internally, we may be dealing with anger, great pain, grief, or brokenness over the first evil that happened to us. This leaves us unable to move on, experience joy, or be in healthy relationships. To further complicate the situations, we may make poor life choices while in our state of desolation.

Identify Entry Points

The first evil or hurt perpetrated against you can result in an open door or entry point into your life. It can open the door for a lie to come in and insert itself in your life or mind. This entry point can be the start of a poor image, false perception, or insecurity. If this lie is not dealt with, it can become a stronghold where a person can remain in a state of desolation for a long period of time. For example, if a teenager is abused and the abuser tells her that it is all her fault, "You deserve to be abused," that act of abuse and words spoken create an entry point for the lie. If the lie is believed, then the teenager may choose to accept other abuse or abusive situations in her life, all the while thinking that she deserves it. The state of desolation for this teenager is that she believes the lie that the abuse she suffers is all her fault. She will continue to find herself in abusive situations and will not think to stand up for herself because she has believed the lie that she deserves it. This thought process is reflective in many areas of her life; even as an adult, she may be mistreated by a spouse or coworker. So now, the teenager has grown into an adult, limping through life in this state of desolation, and it all started with the first incident of abuse where the lie first entered. To overcome this cycle, the teen or adult must identify the initial entry point and replace the lie with a truth from Scripture.

This is an example:

Lie: It is my fault that bad things, like abuse, happen to me.
Replace with truth: But each one is tempted when he is drawn away by his own desires and enticed. (James 1:14)
I did not cause somebody to sin against me or harm me. They did it because of the evil in their own heart.

Example #2:

Lie: I deserve to be mistreated. I must not be worthy of proper treatment.

Replace with truth: For You formed my inward parts; You covered me in my mother's womb. I will praise You, for I am fearfully and wonderfully made. (Psalm 139:13,14)

God does not create trash. I am valuable and should be treated with value.

Jephthah, Stuck in the State of Desolation

Jephthah is an Old Testament character in the Bible who was stuck in a state of desolation until he finally confronted the original hurt or first evil in his life. In Judges 11:1-3 it says:

Now Jephthah the Gileadite was a mighty man of valor, but he was the son of a harlot; and Gilead begot Jephthah. Gilead's wife bore sons; and when his wife's sons grew up, they drove Jephthah out, and said to him, "You shall have no inheritance in our father's house, for you are the son of another woman. Then Jephthah fled from his brothers and dwelt in the land of Tob; and worthless men banded together with Jephthah and went out raiding with him.

How others saw and treated Jephthah affected how he began to think and act. Jephthah must have felt worthless after his brothers treated him like it, throwing him out and cheating him of his inheritance. They said he did not deserve the inheritance—that essentially, he deserved to be mistreated instead. He then attracted men that acted how he saw and felt about himself. Jephthah believed the lie that his family or circumstances perpetrated against him that he was worthless, so he surrounded himself with worthless men and carried out worthless deeds, stealing from others. If you continue to read the story, you will learn that fortunately, Jephthah did redeem himself after he confronted his family for mistreating him (Judg. 11:7). Perhaps you attract what you are or believe about yourself. If you believe what others say about you, you will likely fulfill their words and actions.

Stuck in the State of Desolation

It is easy to see how victims of sexual abuse, especially childhood sexual abuse, will carry their hurt into their future without even realizing it. If an individual's boundaries are violated, it may be hard for him or her to enforce boundaries in future relationships. How does one rebuild a boundary after it has been violated and torn down? Without a healthy boundary in place, one may not even recognize the warning signs of danger in a new relationship. Perhaps during the first evil or the hurt perpetrated against you you learned to be silent; you lost your voice to stand up and speak for yourself. All these things could make you more vulnerable to re-victimization until you are able to establish a boundary.

Often times, an individual can experience depression or anxiety or even suffer from post-traumatic stress disorder from the first evil or hurt. How do you deal with trauma? Are you self-medicating with illegal drugs or alcohol to numb the trauma and bad memories of the first evil or hurt? Other negative coping behaviors could involve various addictions that ease your pain, such as eating disorders, self-injury, or shopping binges, but these are all followed by feelings of regret. What poor choices have you made in your state of desolation?

A Modern-Day Tamar

Tammy's life had changed a lot since prom night. Bryan had indeed taken nude pictures of her and even circulated them to his friends. It spread fast, and before she knew it, everybody was looking at her differently. She felt constantly violated every time that she would walk into a room, and the guys would all sneer at her and make comments about her body. She became withdrawn, and instead of enjoying social activities with classmates, she now wanted to be alone at home, away from all the chatter. At first, she had hoped that everything would blow over after a couple of days, but people continued to talk about her. People that she had been friends with for years now suddenly seemed to avoid her, as if they were ashamed to be around her or admit they were friends with her. Even Jake and other guys that were truly gentlemen dismissed her as if she was now disqualified from being with them. She felt everybody's rejection, as if she was trash now to be only discarded.

She even heard that Bryan had sent the photos to some friends at the state university. It seemed that she would never be able to get past what happened to her that night. Now the last thing she wanted to do was leave the safety of her home and go away to the state university where people were already talking about her. She decided to stay home and attend the local community college. She began to think that perhaps she deserved this; she should have never gone to the party to begin with. She was never able to explain to her parents what happened that night, and she only hoped that they would never see the pictures of her. They would never understand. Now, they just seemed disappointed with her and every decision that she made.

Questions Chapter Two

Tamar's Story:

1. What were Amnon's feelings toward Tamar after forcing himself on her?

_____

_____

_____

2. How do you think Tamar felt after Amnon forced her?

_____

_____

_____

3. What do you think Tamar meant when she said, "The evil of sending me away is worse than the other (evil) that you did to me?"

_____

_____

_____

4. Why did Tamar put ashes on her head and tear her robe?

_____

_____

_____

5. Why do you think Tamar depended on her brother Absalom to provide for her?

_____

_____

_____

6. For purposes of this workbook, what does the phrase "state of desolation" mean?

_____

_____

_____

7. What was Tamar's state of desolation?

_____

_____

_____

Jephthah's story:

8. What was Jephthah's state of desolation, and what illegal act did he carry out in that frame of mind?

_____

_____

_____

A Place to Take Your Shame

Your Story:

9. What was your hurt or the first evil that happened to you? (Remember, this does not have to be one event. It could be several years of abuse. If you need more space than is provided here in this workbook, you may want to purchase a journal and enter the answers to these questions there.)

_____

_____

_____

_____

10. In your life, was there a second evil involved, a consequence that hurt more than the first evil? (ex. being rejected by family, nobody believing or supporting you)

_____

_____

_____

_____

11. Are you stuck in a state of desolation or false self-perception?

_____

_____

_____

12. If so, identify the lies you have believed; often times, this requires going back to their entry point. Then, find scriptures to replace the lies. You may only have one or several. One alone can cause years of hurt. Please take the time to identify every lie you have believed so that you

can replace it with a truth from Scripture. (Do this on a separate sheet of paper or in a separate journal, not where the entries of your hurts are recorded. I encourage you to keep this answer to review or memorize later.)

Lie: _____

_____

Truth: _____

_____

Closing Prayer: If you have made poor choices in your state of desolation, pray that the Lord would help you to make positive choices with the truth that you now have. He is the master at turning something meant to destroy you into something beautiful (Gen. 50:20, Rom. 8:28).

Chapter Three

A FATHER'S RESPONSE

2 Samuel 13:21-22
But when King David heard of all these things, he was very angry. And Absalom spoke to his brother Amnon neither good nor bad. For Absalom hated Amnon, because he had forced his sister Tamar.

Tamar Never Returned to the Palace

Tamar never returned to the palace. Her home was not the place she went to seek safety and shelter. What would she say if the other virgin daughters, her half-sisters, asked where her robe was and why she wasn't wearing it anymore? What could she possibly say to explain why she wasn't a virgin anymore? She must have felt too unworthy to return to the palace, just as she felt too unworthy to wear the beautiful robe. And even if she did return, what would she now have in common with her half-sisters? She was no longer waiting to be given in marriage, as they were. She could no longer be courted by prosperous young men, like her sisters were.

At this time, her father, King David was the most powerful man in the nation of Israel. The law required that Amnon be punished by death for his actions, as the Scripture explains in Deuteronomy 22. King David had authority as a father over his son to bring punishment upon Amnon. Also, as Tamar's father, it was his responsibility to see that justice was rendered on her behalf. Furthermore, as king, David had government authority to see that punishment according to the law was carried out upon Amnon. David did not act in his role as father or king to see that Tamar received justice and Amnon was punished for his crime.

There is nothing in Scripture that says or even implies that David went to his daughter to comfort her or invite her back to her rightful place in the palace. He seemed fine to allow her to remain desolate in her brother's house, hiding in shame and pain. David's silence and lack of action could only be perceived by Tamar as great rejection. If I was in Tamar's situation, I would probably feel deeply wounded by his lack of action. How could the person that was supposed to defend me sit by and do nothing?

What Tamar may not have known was David's own childhood story, how he himself was rejected by his own father when he was a child. David's father, Jesse, gave him the lowest job of being a shepherd. When the prophet Samuel came to anoint one of Jesse's sons to be the next king in Israel, Jesse did not think highly enough of David to include him with all his other sons to present before Samuel. Later in Chapter 5, we will visit the reality of dysfunction that is passed from one generation to the next and how that cycle can be broken. Also, David's own sexual misconduct may have been the seed that started all these events that unfolded in Tamar's life, as the prophet Nathan declared to David in 2 Samuel 12:10, that "the sword shall never depart from your house."

These two points about David are only to state that his silence to Tamar may not have been about her but more about the internal conflict and issues in his own heart. Every time he thought about what happened to Tamar, he may have felt personal guilt because of his own sexual sin and the prophecy or punishment concerning it. Her suffering may have been a reminder of his own mistakes—how could he look at her without being reminded of his own guilt and sin? How could he punish his son for sexual sin when he too in his past was guilty of sexual sin?

A Father's Response

Similarly, in your situation, you may be perceiving the lack of support that you received as personal rejection. In reality, it has less to do with you and more to do with the other person and the issues or conflict in his or her own heart. Perhaps they too, like David, have past sin in their lives that they are ashamed of. Maybe looking at you is a reminder to them of their own flaws and shortcomings. Are you disappointed because you experienced a lack of support? If so, it is important that you don't receive that as personal rejection. Instead, you should understand that the lack of support you received likely has less to do with you and more to do with the people who failed to give it.

Do you feel like Tamar? Have you felt that you are the one that is rejected and shunned from your family since the abuse? A father's response, like David's, often has to do with his own issues more than you or yours. If your father didn't respond in love out of care and protection for you, don't allow his issue to become yours. Sometimes, it is harder to release and forgive the person that was supposed to protect and defend us than it is to forgive the person that actually perpetrated the abuse. For example, a parent who looks away when a friend of the family abuses his or her child or refuses to believe the child after the child tells would be considered an enabler to the abuser. It is worth noting that sometimes it is best not to be reunited with family. If the family continues to display abusive behavior, then being separated from them is best.

Tamar is Avenged

Since David himself fell into sexual sin with Bathsheba, perhaps this is why he couldn't bring himself to punish his son Amnon for something he was once guilty of himself. Absalom, being the oldest son and Tamar's full brother, decided to fulfill the legal obligation that his father, King David, would not. After two years, Absalom rose up and killed Amnon. Justice was finally rendered, but it did come at a high price. David's family indeed was divided by the sword and was torn apart. The only comfort that Tamar seemed to have was from her brother Absalom who provided for her. As a result of Absalom killing Amnon, he had to flee the country, thus isolating Tamar even more.

Choose to Trust in Your Heavenly Father

We all have a Creator, a Father in heaven who formed us in our mother's womb. When God formed man and woman, He created us with the gift of free will, which means we can choose life or choose death. Everyone can choose for themselves. God will not force His will on anybody. Sadly, when one individual chooses to harm or sin against another, God will not override his or her gift of free will, thus forcing His will on somebody. Even though it is not God's desire to see man harming one other and sinning against each other, He allows it to happen. Our heavenly Father will not violate His own principle when He established giving men free will. As a result of this, we sometimes mistake God's silence as being angry or powerless toward us. Each person at some point in his or her journey must resolve the question, where was God when _____ happened to me? You fill in the blank. Where was God when the first evil was perpetrated against me?

There is a story in the Bible that reconciles this question for us all. The story of Joseph can be found in Genesis chapters 37-50. Joseph was abused by his older brothers because of their jealousy towards him. Not only did they throw him in a pit and tell their father that he was dead, but they sold him into slavery. Today, this would be considered human trafficking. Joseph came to a profound conclusion several years later in Genesis 50:20 (NKJV) when he said to his brothers, "But as for you, you meant evil against me; but God meant it for good, in order to bring it about as it is this day, to save many people alive." What has happened to you? Can you come to an understanding that your hurt and abuse was not God's will or heart toward you? God is a good heavenly Father that loves you. Somebody sinned against you because of the evil in his or her own heart, knowing that it would hurt you. God allowed it to happen because He will not violate His own principles of free will that He established for each person. However, God also knew from the beginning how He could work in your situation and have it work out for a greater good. But you must choose to invite God into your situation, surrendering to Him the hurt that others did to you. None of us are defined by what happens to us at the hands of others because God's plan and purpose for us cannot be thwarted by another's sin.

Our Heavenly Father is not like our Earthly Father

The idea that God is our heavenly Father may be hard for us to grasp. Often times, we are set up to view our heavenly Father based on the type of earthly father we have. If your earthly father was a positive influence in your life, then accepting God as your heavenly Father will be easier for you than someone who has hurt or unresolved issues with his or her earthly father. Matthew 7:9-11(NKJV) says, "Or what man is there among you who, if his son asks for bread, will give him a stone? Or if he asks for a fish, will he give him a serpent? If you then, being evil, know how to give good gifts to your children, how much more will your Father who is in heaven give good things to those who ask Him!"

Regardless of your experience with your earthly father, know that your heavenly Father is good and desires to give you good things. God's plans for you are good, not evil. If you have never accepted Jesus into your heart to be your Father and Lord, I encourage you to do so now by saying this prayer: God, You did not cause the bad or hurtful things in my life. They were not your will or your heart toward me. I will not blame You or be mad at You for anything others have chosen to do to me. I am not perfect and would like to have a fresh start. I would like to have peace. I believe that You love me so much that you sent your Son, Jesus, to die on a cross for my sins. I accept what Jesus did on the cross as payment for my sins. I want You to live in my heart and help me make better decisions that will please You. In Jesus's name, I pray and ask this. Amen.

A Place to Take Your Shame

A Modern-Day Tamar

Tammy was able to take courses at her local community college, but her parents did require her to obtain a job. Shortly after starting her job, she began a relationship with one of her older coworkers, Tom. He was new in town and did not seem to have heard or seen any of the pictures concerning her and that awful night. She knew that Tom was not the type that her dad would approve of, but he was always nice to her. Although at times, he did seem too jealous whenever she was simply having a work-related conversation with another coworker that happened to be male. She became very close with Tom very fast. It was nice to not feel rejected and have somebody that she could trust and talk to. She probably should have seen some warning signs that Tom was becoming too possessive of her. Before she realized it, the relationship had become too serious too fast. Feeling that she had limited options when she became pregnant, she moved in with him. This was just another choice in a long list of things that disappointed her parents. As time passed, she hated to admit it, but her mother was right; after the birth of their child, she stopped going to college.

Questions Chapter Three

Tamar's Consequences:

1. What was King David's response to Tamar when he heard she was raped?

_____

_____

_____

2. Why do you think Tamar did not return to the palace?

_____

_____

_____

3. Why couldn't Tamar be given in marriage?

_____

_____

_____

David's Choices:

4. Describe the relationship King David had with his father when he was a child:

_____

_____

_____

5. Why did the prophet Nathan declare to David that the sword would not depart from his home?

_____
_____
_____

Amnon's Consequences:

6. What was King David's response to Amnon when he heard that he had raped his daughter Tamar?

_____
_____
_____

7. What did the law of their day say should have happened to Amnon?

_____
_____
_____

8. What eventually happened to Amnon?

_____
_____
_____

9. Why was Absalom forced to flee the nation and live away from his family?

_____

_____

_____

Reflecting Inwardly:

10. What has God given each of us that allows us to sin or not sin?

_____

_____

_____

11. What happened to Joseph? And what conclusion did he reach concerning the evil intended to harm him?

_____

_____

_____

_____

12. Like Joseph, are you able to reach a similar conclusion concerning the evil intended to harm you?

_____

_____

_____

A Place to Take Your Shame

13. According to the Bible, how is your heavenly Father compared to your earthly father?

_____

_____

_____

Closing Prayer: Have you accepted Jesus, your good heavenly Father, into your heart? If not, pray this prayer: God, You did not cause the bad or hurtful things in my life. They were not your will or your heart toward me. I will not blame You or be mad at You for anything others have chosen to do to me. I am not perfect and would like to have a fresh start. I would like to have peace. I believe that You love me so much that You sent your Son, Jesus, to die on a cross for my sins. I accept what Jesus did on the cross as payment for my sins. I want You to live in my heart and help me to make better decisions that will please You. In Jesus's name, I pray and ask this. Amen.

Chapter Four

CHOOSE TO FORGIVE

In life, it is not so much what happens to you, because you can be certain that we will all at some time experience trauma, pain, or injustice, but what matters most is how you choose to respond to what happens to you.

What is Forgiveness

Forgiveness is to let go, release, or dismiss somebody from a debt owed. According to Strong's Exhaustive Concordance of the Bible, the word forgiveness from Ephesians 1:7, means "freedom, pardon, deliverance, forgiveness, liberty, and remission." Usage for the word "forgive" taken from Matthew 18:35, is described by Strong's Concordance as "I send away, I let go, release, I permit to depart, I remit, forgive." The above definitions look at the original Greek language to better describe the meaning of the word forgiveness used in these two scriptures. It helps give us a clear understanding of what forgiveness is and looks like. Place the name of the abuser and enabler and apply it to these definitions. For example, "I forgive, pardon, send away, let go, release, remit _____ from any debt owed to me."

Myths about Forgiveness

Myth #1
Forgiveness says that everything is okay, that what happened to me was no big deal; and therefore, if I have forgiven, then there should be no consequence for the abuser.

FALSE: Forgiveness is not dismissing the act that was committed against you, nor is it saying that it was okay to abuse you. Forgiveness simply says that you will not be held in bondage to that act. One can forgive but still seek justice at the same time. Forgiving and wanting justice are two different things and cannot be confused as the same thing.

Myth #2
If I have truly forgiven, then I will forget too.

FALSE: You can forgive the person, but you will not be able to forget the act that was committed against you. Allow this to be a defense mechanism; a memory can give you wisdom or self-preservation. Just because you have forgiven the abuser does not mean that you should allow yourself to be alone with them or in any vulnerable situation with them. Forgiveness is what is needed here, but do not take on the responsibility of trying to minister to them in a way that would jeopardize your safety.

Myth #3
Forgiveness is hard and hurts the victim; the abuser does not deserve my forgiveness.

FALSE: Many times, the abuser is unaware of the victim's pain and unforgiveness. The burden of unforgiveness hurts the victim more than the abuser. Unforgiveness will drown out love, and it can take over all other emotions. Unforgiveness can consume you, especially when it turns to bitterness and anger. There is torment in unforgiveness. The abuser may never ask for your forgiveness, but you should forgive anyway.

Myth #4
I must have revenge. Revenge will give me peace, vindicate me, and make the wrong that was done to me right.

FALSE: Revenge does not bring peace, and it will not change or take the pain of what happened to you away. When you forgive, you are putting the abuser into the hands of the Lord. God will deal with him or her as He sees fit. In Romans 12:19, the Bible tells us that vengeance belongs to the Lord.

What Scripture says about Forgiveness
Jesus said the following about forgiveness in Matthew 18:21-35 (NKJV):
21 Then Peter came to Him and said, "Lord, how often shall my brother sin against me, and I forgive him? Up to seven times?"
22 Jesus said to him, "I do not say to you, up to seven times, but up to seventy times seven. 23 Therefore the kingdom of heaven is like a certain king who wanted to settle accounts with his servants. 24 And when he had begun to settle accounts, one was brought to him who owed him ten thousand talents. 25 But as he was not able to pay, his master commanded that he be sold, with his wife and children and all that he had, and that payment be made. 26 The servant therefore fell down before him, saying, 'Master, have patience with me, and I will pay you all.' 27 Then the master of that servant was moved with compassion, released him, and forgave him the debt.
28 "But that servant went out and found one of his fellow servants who owed him a hundred denarii; and he laid hands on him and took him by the throat, saying, 'Pay me what you owe!' 29 So his fellow servant fell down at his feet and begged him, saying, 'Have patience with me, and I will pay you all.' 30 And he would not, but went and threw him into prison till he should pay the debt. 31 So when his fellow servants saw what had been done, they were very grieved, and came and told their master all that had been done. 32 Then his master, after he had called him, said to him, 'You wicked servant! I forgave you all that debt

because you begged me. 33 Should you not also have had compassion on your fellow servant, just as I had pity on you?' 34 And his master was angry, and delivered him to the torturers until he should pay all that was due to him.

35 "So My heavenly Father also will do to you if each of you, from his heart, does not forgive his brother his trespasses."

We are commanded to forgive. As we read in the above verses, Jesus Himself commands us to forgive if we want to be forgiven by God, our heavenly Father. Who do you need to forgive, your abuser or an enabler in the situation? Do you need to forgive yourself? Have you been punishing yourself for something that was not your fault? Forgiving yourself can prove to be the most challenging hurdle. Have you been angry with God and perhaps falsely blamed Him? Maybe you need to forgive God.

Three things to stay in a place of forgiveness
1. Pray for those whom you need to forgive.

   Luke 6:27-28 But I say to you who hear: Love your enemies, do good to those who hate you, bless those who curse you, and pray for those who spitefully use you.

   As you pray for the person or those involved that wounded you, you will get an eternal perspective on their souls. You will not see them for the horrible act or acts that they did but as lost souls on their way to hell unless they repent. Nobody deserves eternity in hell. Pray for others who can witness and minister to them.

2. Forgiveness is more than a one-time event.

   Once you have chosen to forgive your abuser or those involved in hurting you, feelings of frustration and anger may still linger. Forgiveness is not a decision you make only one time but an ongoing decision you must make consistently. For example, after completing this chapter, you decide to forgive your stepfather who abused you. Then three days later, feelings of anger and resentment toward him come back to you. As soon as you experience those feelings, choose to forgive again. Don't dwell on the anger for even a minute. Immediately pray and say, "I choose to forgive." Forgiveness is a consistent action we will have to choose to participate in if we are to do the will of God in our lives.

Ephesians 4:26-27 Be angry, and do not sin. do not let the sun go down on your wrath, nor give place to the devil.

Do not dwell on anger or rehearse the abusive situation over and over in your mind. If you do, you will be allowing the devil a place in your heart and in your life.

3. Remember that forgiveness is a choice. Nobody can force you to forgive, and nobody can force you not to forgive.

A Modern-Day Tamar

Tammy found an invitation at her front door when she came in from work. The church down the street was doing a big Easter celebration, with some giveaways and fun stuff for her daughter to do. As she was reading through the invitation, she realized it was the same church that one of her coworkers had been inviting her to. Over dinner that night, she mentioned it to Tom, who showed no interest. He said he had plans to sleep in and most likely would be out drinking since he was off work that Monday.

Tammy decided to attend church without Tom and brought her daughter. She was so moved by the service that she went to the front for prayer. She followed through with her plans to go to her mother's house for lunch afterward. When her mother answered the door, Tammy noticed something that she had not before. Life had not been kind to Tammy's mother through the years. After Tammy's father passed unexpectantly, her mother seemed to grow bitter in the years that followed. Financially, she was fine, but she seemed to reflect back on her life with sadness and regret.

Tammy was so excited about her experience that day that she confessed to her mother all that had happened at church. Tammy explained how she felt compelled to forgive others because Jesus forgave her. As her mother stared at her, Tammy continued to talk. She began to confess all the people and things she needed to forgive. She confessed that she felt so much rejection from her parents for not going away to the state university and dropping out even at the local community college. She said to her mother, "I know you are disappointed in me and how my life turned out because of my decisions."

Her mother cried and said, "I love you; I just wanted better for you. I didn't want you to feel stuck like I did all these years. See, I didn't have the best relationship with my parents. My stepfather was cruel to me at times. I became involved with your father too soon and became pregnant with you before I was ready to be a mother. But I quickly married your father because he provided a way for me to move out of my parents' home. At the time, I never imagined that your father would be so controlling and verbally and emotionally abusive all those years. I thought that because he didn't hit me, unlike my stepfather, everything would be good. I see now that your father's behavior was abusive toward me and even you at times. I'm sorry that it's taken me this long to realize. Please forgive me." While her mother spoke, Tammy replayed memories of her childhood in her mind—her parents' marriage, events, and comments that had gone unnoticed now shone brightly in her memory. Looking at her mother, Tammy said, "I forgive you, Mom."

Questions Chapter Four

Personal Application:

1. What does forgiveness mean?

_____

_____

_____

2. What are the four false myths about forgiveness?

_____

_____

_____

3. Do you struggle with any of those myths; if so, why?

_____

_____

_____

4. According to Romans 12:19, who does vengeance belong to?

_____

_____

_____

5. Who commands us to forgive?

_____

_____

_____

6. Who do you need to forgive?

_____

_____

7. Place their names in the lines below:

I forgive _____.
I pardon _____.
I release _____from any debt they owe me.
I dismiss _____from anything owed to me.
I will choose to let _____go.
I send _____away and permit them to depart from me.
I no longer want to be tied to this person or event.
Repeat the above out loud as many times as you need to.

8. Understanding what three things will help you to stay in a place of forgiveness?

_____

_____

_____

9. Will you spend time every day for the next week praying for the soul of the person(s) that you need to forgive?

_____

_____

_____

10. Who are you giving a place to in your heart and life if you remain angry?

_____

_____

_____

Closing Prayer: Lord, please help me to forgive those that hurt me. I do not want to be tied to them or the hurt that they perpetrated against me. Help me to forgive and walk in freedom every day. In Jesus's name, Amen.

Chapter Five

GRIEVE THE LOSS & BREAK THE CYCLE

What was Lost

Tamar was a princess, so people treated her with great respect. Everything changed for her the minute she was raped. In that act, she lost many things—innocence, dignity, self-esteem, and her future plans of marriage. After the first evil was perpetrated against you, what do you feel you lost? Do you feel your childhood innocence or self-worth was robbed?

Just as Tamar could no longer look forward to being given in marriage, perhaps you lost your dream of that perfect wedding because you feel undeserving of that now. You may feel through what happened to you that you lost your voice or ability to speak up for yourself. How long did you remain in a "state of desolation?" In that state or frame of mind, you may have chosen to engage in destructive behavior that you regret now. Things that you now see as valuable, you may have freely given away or wasted. All these things were lost. I recommend that you take an honest look at your life and begin a list of what was lost. Now that you have identified your loss, it is time to grieve that loss.

Grieve the Loss

It may seem silly to go back and cry over something that happened a long time ago, but sometimes we must go backward before we can go forward. It is necessary to take this step of grieving so that you may overcome all that was lost once and for all.

In the Bible, grieving is described as mourning, weeping, or bewailing. During biblical times, when somebody was grieving, they often tore their clothes, put on sackcloth and ashes, tore their hair, or beat their chest. Immediately after Tamar was raped and put of the house, she tore her robe and put ashes on her head. An outward sign is not required if you are mourning inwardly, though. You can be mourning and sorrowful in heart and spirit but not showing it outwardly. Different people may grieve in different ways; while some may cry, others may not. Most people grieving in today's society will have to continue their daily routines and commitments while they are grieving, and that is certainly understandable.

Now that you have identified what was lost, you must grieve it. Grieving will not change your past but will hopefully help you heal from it and begin to put it completely behind you. This is not to say that you should have a pity party or feel sorry for yourself. Talking about your grief for a long period of time until you fall into a depression will certainly not help matters. Rather, you must go backward temporarily so that ultimately, you can go forward and never look back again. This step in the process is not to have you stay in the past; this is why you will be asked to set an appointed time to grieve, and when that time is up, you will grieve no more.

Biblical Examples of Grieving

Biblical grieving was for a season or appointed time that was pre-determined. You should not think or say to yourself, "I will stop grieving when I feel better about the situation." Ecclesiastes 3:1 says, "To everything there is a season, a time for every purpose under heaven." Ecclesiastes 3:4 says, "A time to weep, and a time to laugh. A time to mourn, and a time to dance." There is a purpose for your season, even a season of grieving. The purpose is to give you closure over your loss. Psalm 30:5 says, "Weeping may endure for a night. But joy comes in the morning."

When your appointed time and purpose for grieving is fulfilled, then it is time to move on. Deuteronomy 34:8 says, "And the children of Israel wept for Moses in the plains of Moab thirty days. So the days of weeping and mourning for Moses ended." Notice here that the people did not grieve past the appointed time of thirty days. The grieving was for an appointed time to fulfill a purpose. In 1 Samuel 16:1, we see a situation where God confronted the prophet Samuel because he continued to mourn for something that he could not change. This is a lesson to us all that we cannot stay in a prolonged state of grief because we cannot go back and change what has already happened. Therefore, when the appointed time to grieve is up, we must move forward.

Remember when you are grieving over your list that if something on the list was the loss of a dream or the loss of something you will never get to experience, that is biblical too. Judges 11:34-40 tells the story of a young girl who would never be married so she grieved the loss of what she would never get to experience for the appointed time of two months.

Now that you have your list of losses and understand that grieving is for an appointed time, determine the appointed time that you will grieve. A recommendation is about two weeks. This varies for each person and the situation he or she may be grieving over. If you have a very long list of things that must be grieved, then you may want to grieve longer; however, it is not recommended to grieve for over a month. Where situations vary, others may feel that two days is a long enough time to grieve. This is a personal decision. It is very important that once your appointed time for grieving is up, you move on. You can start grieving when you are finished with this chapter. Some may complete this workbook before their appointed time of grieving is over, and that is fine too.

Stuck in a Cycle or Pattern

How do you know if it is just life circumstances or coincidence or if you are really stuck in a cycle? If you're wondering what I am talking about, let me give you an example to help illustrate my question. A young girl grows up in a home where her father is an alcoholic. When he gets drunk, he becomes very angry and takes his anger out on both her and her mother. He is harsh and unloving and often times can't remember the things he said and did while he was drunk. The daughter grows up in this environment and sees the hurt it causes her and her mother. She swears for years to her mother and her friends that when she is older, she will not marry an alcoholic like her father. She explains that she does not want to relive the hurt she has already experienced in her childhood. However, when she is older, several years later, she somehow finds herself married to an alcoholic, reliving the same hurts of her childhood. Perhaps I am not the only one who has seen or heard these scenarios and wondered the following: How did this happen? Did she unknowingly learn some type of behavior as a child that caused her to marry an alcoholic as an adult? Was she attracted to or drawn to what was most familiar to her? Or was this the result of some type of curse that both she and her mother suffered from? Let's look at both of these possibilities.

Learned Behavior

There may be some subconscious learned behaviors that you do in your life without even realizing it. Let's break this down. The word "subconscious" is defined by The Cambridge Dictionary as "relating to thoughts and feelings that exist in the mind and influence your behavior although you are not aware of them." In other words, you don't know why you do these behaviors, but you do. It is almost like a knee-jerk reaction. It comes naturally to you. Here's an example of this. A young woman who was recently married decided to have the traditional Thanksgiving meal at her new home. With all the generations represented at the table, herself and her husband along with her mother and grandmother and their husbands, she placed the large pan on the table, and the turkey was cut in half. Her husband asked, "Why is the turkey cut in half?" The newly-married woman, cooking this traditional meal on her own for the first time, replied, "I am not sure. As a little girl, I always remember watching my mother cut the turkey in half before putting it in the pan and baking it." Everybody at the table looked at her mother, who gave the exact same response. Everybody then turned to the grandmother, who responded by saying, "In my day, I didn't own a pan large enough for the whole turkey; therefore, I cut it in half and placed it in my small pan before baking it. But concerning my daughter and her daughter, I'm not sure why they do this since they do own pans large enough!" This story illustrates a learned behavior that became a habit passed from one generation to the next. The young daughter and her mother continued this behavior until somebody questioned it.

I am asking you to take some time to question some of your behaviors. Take an honest assessment and look at your life and the decisions you make. Why do you make those decisions? Is there a buried learned behavior that you have not realized until this moment of self-reflection and questioning? The above story is humorous, but there can be some learned behaviors buried in your subconscious that were passed down but have serious consequences. So, it is important that you take this time of self-reflection and questioning seriously, particularly as it relates to behaviors that are negative or result in destructive outcomes. Ask the Lord to open your eyes and help reveal these to you.

Follow these steps during your time of self-reflection:
- Create a list writing out any toxic or negative behaviors that you participate in.
- Ask yourself when was the first time you caught yourself doing this and what provoked you to do it, or what thoughts did you initially have while doing it?

- Now that you have identified these negative learned behaviors, you must change them or unlearn them. To effectively stop doing them, it is best to replace each with a positive behavior.
- For some, it may help to revisit question 12 from chapter 2. Some of your negative behaviors may be the result of a lie believed. If so, next to the lie add the negative behavior that results. Then, where you have already found a truth from Scripture, add the new positive behavior next to it that will be replacing the negative behavior.

Lie: You are nothing but an accident; nothing good will ever come of you.

Negative Learned Behavior: Since there is no purpose for my life, I cannot expect anything good to happen to me. There is no point in applying for college or a scholarship. Mistakes and accidents like me don't get those good opportunities.

Replace with Truth: For I know the thoughts that I think toward you, says the Lord, thoughts of peace and not evil, to give you a future and a hope. (Jeremiah 29:11)

Replace with Positive Behavior: I choose to believe that with God's help, my life can change, and good things can happen to and through me. Therefore, I will apply for the college and the scholarship.

- If your negative learned behavior is not associated with a lie, I encourage you to complete the following exercise:

Negative Behavior: Finding yourself in abusive relationships with men that will not marry you or treat you with respect.

Positive Replacement Behavior: Abstain from sexual relations and demonstrate behavior that commands respect.

Empowerment Scriptures to help you do this: I can do all things through Christ who strengthens me. (Philippians 4:13) But Jesus looked at them and said to them, "With men this is impossible, but with God all things are possible.'" (Matthew 19:26)

The empowerment scriptures listed can be applied for many different situations, and I encourage you to use them as often as needed. This simple exercise may only be scratching the surface. For some reading, there may be a long list of very destructive behaviors that have now woven a very thick and tangled web that will take a while to unravel. Behaviors that have been modeled and practiced over a lifetime are not unlearned over one night, so be persistent. Ask the Lord to strengthen and empower you while you go through this process.

Generational Curses

There is a spiritual principle, whether you realize it or not, that may not be working in your favor right now. Exodus 20:5 says, "You shall not bow down to them nor serve them (idols.) For I, the Lord your God, *am* a jealous God, visiting the iniquity of the fathers upon the children to the third and fourth *generations* of those who hate Me." This text has to do with the Ten Commandments, but there is a principle that if the commandments are not kept, God will visit the children and their children's children of those who break His commandments. However, Jesus gave His life (body and blood) for us all who have sinned. So, when we accept Jesus into our hearts and lives, we accept the price He paid as payment for the curse or law that was written against us. Many have different opinions on what our responsibility is concerning this curse. Most do not deny there is a curse as mentioned in the above scripture. The debate is concerning when the curse will be broken. Some believe it is immediately broken the minute we accept Jesus into our hearts and become born-again believers. Others believe it is not broken until we verbally renounce all that our fathers and ancestors did. For the purposes of this workbook, I will not argue this debate either way. If you are concerned that you are still being affected by something your relatives did, all you have to do is pray this simple prayer: Lord, please forgive my parents and the generations before them for engaging in any kind of sin. I renounce any kind of sin they may have been involved in. I choose to turn away from that and repent. I do not desire to knowingly or unknowingly be in any kind of sin. Please reveal to me anything that I need to change in my life and give me the strength to do it, in Jesus name, Amen.

Apply Both Solutions

Both possibilities, a generational curse or learned behavior, could be keeping you in a negative cycle. It could even be both of these working together. You may not even be able to separate one from the other. Therefore, I think it is best to apply the solutions to both, the curse and learned behavior, to ensure the cycle is broken. Pray the above suggested prayer to break any possible curse but also pray the Lord will strengthen you to learn new healthy behaviors that line up with His principles.

Also, remember that what is familiar to you may be comforting, even if it is not healthy. As humans, we are creatures of habit. Most of us tend to be drawn to what we know. It can be a scary thing to leave behind what is familiar, even if it is negative, for what is unknown. I personally feel comfortable speaking to this issue because as a young woman, I knew that the women on both sides of my family had not finished high school or gone to college. I was able to break this cycle and obtain two master's degrees, debt-free. I applied both solutions just like I am recommending for you to do also. The example of a lie that resulted in a learned negative behavior that I had to replace with a truth from Scripture and a positive behavior is just one example from my own personal journal.

Tammy Breaks the Cycle

It had been a year since Tammy attended that Easter service. As Easter was nearing again, she continued to pray for Tom, in hopes that he would attend church with her. Church had now become an important part of her life, though it was not a part that Tom shared with her. Tammy was even able to get her mother attending church with her. Tammy not only enjoyed attending church but also the weekly Bible study for mothers. One morning at this study, there was a guest speaker that shared her testimony about being stuck in a cycle of abuse and how God helped her out of it. She purchased the workbook the speaker had written and began praying, "Lord, reveal to me any cycles of sin that I am stuck in and help me overcome." She soon came to realize that her life with Tom was not God's best for her. He was constantly putting her down for her lack of education and church attendance. As Tammy reflected on what she felt God had shown her, she felt despair and assumed that it was too late for her to live the life she had once hoped. But, she wanted things to be different for her daughter.

Later that week, Tammy was cleaning the house before Tom came home. She was trying to vacuum, but her daughter kept running around in front of it. She asked her to stay in her bedroom until the vacuuming was done. About five minutes later, Tom came in from work and headed to their bedroom to shower, like he usually did after work. As soon as Tammy turned the vacuum cleaner off, she heard Tom yelling from the bedroom, followed by her daughter screaming. Tammy ran back just in time to see Tom slapping their daughter hard across the face. Tom just continued to yell, "I've told you not to get into my work travel bag!" Tammy saw that his bag was all dumped out and that there were women's belongings in the bag—only, they weren't her belongings.

At that moment, Tammy realized that Tom was not going to stop being with other women because she had caught him in this lie before. Perhaps this was why he would never commit to marrying her. She also realized that he was taking his frustration out on their daughter. Tammy began to pack her things up to leave the house, but Tom got physical and grabbed their daughter to try to force Tammy to stay. She was able to get out of the house with her daughter but without her car keys, but she did have her phone in her pocket. Concerned for her daughter's safety, she quickly ran further out into the yard and called the police for help.

Questions Chapter Five

Tamar:

1. How do you think Tamar felt about herself before the rape?

_____

_____

_____

_____

2. How do you think she felt after the rape and rejection? What did she lose when she was raped?

_____

_____

_____

What is Grieving:

3. How did Tamar grieve?

_____

_____

_____

4. All the scriptures below teach us something about grieving. Draw a line from the scripture to the correct statement that it teaches about grieving.

Judges 11:37   God says stop mourning for something you cannot change.

Psalm 30:5   For everything, there is a season.

1 Samuel 16:1   It is okay, biblically, to mourn for something that you will never know or experience.

Ecclesiastes 3:1   Weeping may endure for a night, but joy comes in the morning.

5. Is grieving an inward or outward act?
_____
_____

6. Define grieving in your own words:
_____
_____
_____

7. What scriptures tell us the story of a young girl that grieved for two months for the loss of something that she would never get to experience?
_____
_____

A Place to Take Your Shame

Personal Application:

8. What did you lose when you were violated?

_____

_____

_____

9. How much time will you set aside to grieve these losses? *(Mark on your calendar the date you will stop.)*

_____

_____

_____

10. For each negative behavior that you have identified, determine what positive behavior you will replace it with. (Similar to question 12 in chapter 2, use additional paper. You will want to keep this answer for future studying; therefore, it needs to be separate from your other answers and journal where you have entered your hurts.)

Negative Behavior #1:

_____

_____

_____

Positive Replacement Behavior:

_____

_____

_____

Empowerment Scripture to help you do this:

_____

_____

_____

Negative Behavior #2:

_____

_____

_____

Positive Replacement Behavior:

_____

_____

_____

Empowerment Scripture to help you do this:

_____

_____

_____

Closing Prayer: Lord, please reveal to me any thoughts or behaviors that are contrary to the good plan that You have for my life. Empower and strengthen me to change these behaviors.

Chapter Six

Jesus's Blood Cleanses Me

Psalm 51:10

Create in me a clean heart, O God, and renew a steadfast spirit within me.

The Significance of the Blood

When Jesus died on the cross for your sins and mine, He shed His innocent blood. His blood paid the price for us. There is power in His blood that was shed. It cleanses us and gives us power to overcome sin, the sins that you commit or that are committed against you. Revelation 12:11 says, "And they overcame him (the devil) by the blood of the Lamb (Jesus) and by the word of their testimony, and they did not love their lives to the death."

In the Old Testament, or under the old covenant, when people wanted to be free or forgiven of their sins or acts committed, they had to travel to the temple. Often times, this was a long journey because there was only one temple. God's presence was not available to everybody anywhere because it was confined to the Ark of the Covenant in the temple. Forgiveness was granted after a ceremony that required the priest to slaughter an animal. The New Testament, which is the new covenant, is better and preferred over the old, not because the old is discarded but because Jesus came to fulfill the old covenant laws. Hebrews 9:11-14 explains it this way:

> *But Christ came as High Priest of the good things to come, with the greater and more perfect tabernacle not made with hands, that is, not of this creation. Not with the blood of goats and calves, but with His own blood He entered the Most Holy Place once for all, having obtained eternal redemption. For if the blood of bulls and goats and the ashes of a heifer, sprinkling the unclean, sanctifies for the purifying of the flesh, how much more shall the blood of Christ, who through the eternal Spirit offered Himself without spot to God, cleanse your conscience from dead works to serve the living God?*

No longer allow dead works or sinful acts, such as a sexual violation, to have power over you. You are free from them and free to serve a living God.

Blotted Out
Jesus's death disarmed or took the power away from the grip of sin. Colossians 2:13-15 says:

> *And you, being dead in your trespasses and the uncircumcision of your flesh, He has made alive together with Him, having forgiven you all trespasses, having wiped out the handwriting of requirements that was against us, which was contrary to us. And He has taken it out of the way, having nailed it to the cross. Having disarmed principalities and powers, He made a public spectacle of them, triumphing over them in it.*

Now, I am going to ask you to do an exercise that symbolizes what we have learned. If you have made it to this chapter, then that means you have answered some very difficult questions throughout this workbook. Some of your answers may also have extended into a journal if you ran out of space. (If you have not already done so, please separate question 12 from chapter 2, where you identified lies and replaced them with truths, and question 10 from chapter 5, where you identified negative behaviors and replaced them with positive behaviors. I want to encourage you to keep these two answers so that you can reflect back on them and study them in the future. These answers will help you as you desire to renew your mind and change the trajectory of your life.)

Now, take a red marker, pen, or crayon to symbolize the blood that Jesus shed for you. Gather the answers to your questions from this workbook, including the answers on separate paper or in a journal, where you wrote about the first and second evil committed against you. Write over each answer or write largely over the entire page of answers with the red marker, "Paid in Full by the Blood of Jesus." As you do this, say it out loud. My prayer is that this will help you establish a point in time when closure was received. This is a physical point of contact for your faith. As you write over the workbook answers and journal entries that describe the painful evils committed against you, they will be disarmed of their power over you, now being placed under the blood of Jesus. Jesus's blood blots out what you wrote, and His blood cleanses you from it.

Once you have done this, you are now free from it. It no longer has power over you. It is under the blood of Jesus, never to be returned to again. Do not take the blood of Jesus lightly by placing something under it and then digging it back up later. Jesus shed His blood and gave His life so that we could live freely. I strongly recommend throwing the red-marked pages away so that you are not tempted to reopen the hurts again. In the many years that I have walked girls and women through the process in this workbook, I have watched some come up with very creative ways to part with this chapter in their lives. I have seen some burn the pages. I have seen others throw them over a mountaintop, bury them in the earth, or tie them to a balloon and release. Most simply toss them in the trash. The focus is to physically see and come to a place of closure and finality.

Tammy Breaks the Cycle

After the police arrived, Tammy was able to safely get all of her and her daughter's belongings out of the house. She didn't think it would ever come to this. But she knew that staying with Tom would not be the best decision for her daughter. The police watched her safely drive away, and not knowing where else to go, she headed to her mother's house. At first, she was hesitant to explain to her mother why she was there, but her daughter was still upset and shaken by the events of that night, so Tammy broke down in tears and explained to her mom all that had happened. Her mother took a deep breath and said, "Well, you are always welcome here. In fact, you can move back in your old bedroom." Tammy breathed a sigh of relief and decided they would go to bed and unpack her car and stuff the next morning. It had been a long, eventful day.

The next morning, Tammy and her mother began bringing stuff in from Tammy's car. After finally getting all of her stuff out of the car, she began finding a place for it in her old bedroom. This required her shuffling some furniture around. As she began to slide her old bed to another side of the room, she found an old, crumpled up brochure stuck behind the bed. She picked it up and dusted it off and realized it was a college brochure from the state university she was once so excited about attending years ago. As she dusted it off, she noticed it said something about online courses; she had never noticed this part of the brochure before. Just then, she heard her mother's voice from the hallway. As her mother was approaching the room with one last item from Tammy's car, she said, "You know, if you stay here, your money won't have to go toward rent or childcare because I can take care of your daughter. Is there something you want to do besides work at that restaurant?" Just then, her mother turned the corner to enter the room, and Tammy looked up at her while holding the college brochure.

Instead of answering questions for this chapter, please be sure to complete the exercise of writing over all previous answers and journal entries with a red marker.

Closing Prayer: Lord, thank you for dying on the cross for me so that I could be free of the acts committed against me. Help me to walk in this new found freedom.

Chapter Seven
A New Chapter

2 Corinthians 5:17
Therefore, if anyone is in Christ, he is a new creation; old things have passed away; behold, all things have become new.

The previous chapters in your life are now closed. Do not return to them again. Instead, embrace the new thing God will do in your life. Notice this chapter is very short because you get to decide what you want this next season in your life to look like. I want to challenge you to start a new chapter. God is the master at taking a life that has been broken or shattered by hurt and pain and reconstructing it into something amazing. Dream again and ask the Lord what He has in store for you. Write down your new hopes, desires, and dreams here. If you need a place to start, then look at the questions at the end of this chapter to help get you started.

Questions Chapter Seven

1. According to Scripture, how does God see me?

_____

_____

_____

_____

2. What is God's plan for me?

_____

_____

_____

_____

3. What spiritual disciplines or goals will I set for myself? (ex. reading my Bible daily, finding a church to attend)

_____

_____

_____

_____

Closing Prayer: Lord, what is the good plan that You have for my life? Please reveal it to me.

Answer Key

Chapter One

1. Women could NOT work or own property during O.T. Bible times.
2. Women were provided for by the men in their lives, such as a father, husband, or male child.
3. Fathers most commonly chose a groom for their daughter that was of similar belief system and similar socio-economic status. The groom was required to pay a dowry to the father that proved he could financially provide the lifestyle that his daughter had grown accustomed to.
4. According to Deuteronomy 22:21, the daughter shall be killed for playing the harlot in her father's house.
5. King David
6. Maacah, daughter of Talmai, who was the King of Geshur
7. Amnon and Tamar had different mothers, but King David was the father to both of them. Amnon was Tamar's half-brother.
8. Absalom and Tamar were brother and sister, sharing the same mother, with King David as their father.
9. Tamar enjoyed a lifestyle of royalty since her father was the king and her mother was the princess of another land. She was used to the comforts of a palace. Most likely, she had expensive clothing and possibly servants. She was used to being held in high regard and respect.

10. It is most likely that Tamar would have been given in marriage to a wealthy young man, perhaps even a prince of another land. She would have continued to live lavishly and be in a place of respect or authority.
11. It symbolized her status of royalty and relationship to the king. She was a royal princess in the kingdom, a daughter to the king. It also symbolized her purity as a virgin.
12. Tamar went to Amnon's house out of obedience to her father's request. She was simply doing what her father had asked her to do.
13. She begged him not to rape her. Tamar tried to reason and plead with Amnon. She tried to make him see what the consequences would be for him and for her. She did not want the consequences that she knew would come upon her if he continued; therefore, she even agreed to marry him properly according to tradition if he would spare her from the consequences of rape.
14. No. There is nothing in Scripture that implies or would lead us to believe that Tamar deserved, instigated, or desired this in any way.
15. No. According to this text, a woman that is raped is not to be blamed. She cried for help, but it was not her fault that there was nobody to help her.
16. No. Nobody deserves to be abused or mistreated. Abusive behavior reveals more about the person doing it and the issues of his or her heart than it does the victim.
17. An abuser need not always be physically stronger and exert physical force over the victim. An abuser could be anybody with power over another that chooses to use or abuse that power for his or her sexual desires (boss over an employee, pastor over a member, police officer over a citizen).

Answer Key

Chapter Two

1. After Amnon forced himself on Tamar, he now hated her more than he had once loved her.
2. She probably did not feel like a princess anymore. She probably did not feel worthy of being in the palace or wearing her robe. She may have felt rejection, hurt, and shame.
3. The second (or other) evil of sending her away sentenced her to a life of pain, rejection, and desolation. It forced her to be unmarried and without children. She had to carry and bear the burden of this, forever committing her to a life of shame. This was far worse than the first evil, the actual physical act of rape.
4. She tore her robe because she knew she was no longer worthy to wear it anymore. She was no longer a virgin. Putting ashes on her head symbolized grieving. She immediately began grieving the wrong that was done to her.
5. In Tamar's day, women couldn't work or own property, so she was dependent upon a man to provide for her. She could no longer be given in marriage and expect a husband to provide for her. She would now never have children, so there was no hope of a male child that could provide for her. Her father did not show a desire to visit her, comfort her, or welcome her back into the palace to provide for her. Her brother was most likely the closest male family member to her.
6. For the purposes of this workbook, it means to be without hope or comfort—a frame of mind, a false perception, or way of thinking after the first evil or hurt that happened.
7. Tamar was left in her brother's house without marrying or having children.
8. Jephthah's brothers treated him like he was worthless since his mother was a prostitute. They refused to allow him to have any part in his father's inheritance. As a result, worthless men surrounded themselves around him. It could be said that we attract

what we think about ourselves. They went out and raided others, which is to steal from people.
9. personal answer
10. personal answer
11. personal answer
12. personal answer

Chapter Three

1. King David was angry but not angry enough to carry out the punishment upon his son that was required by law. Also, the Bible never records that David reached out to Tamar to comfort her in anyway. If he had, than it is not likely that she would have remained desolate in her brother's house.
2. How could Tamar hold her head up in the palace? What would she say to her other siblings when they asked where her robe that symbolized her virginity was? Perhaps she did not feel worthy to return.
3. According to the Jewish law and the customs of her day, Tamar could no longer be given in marriage because she was not a virgin.
4. David was rejected by his father, Jesse, who gave him the lowly job of tending to the sheep. He also did not include David when calling for all his other sons to stand before the prophet Samuel.
5. David had committed the sin of adultery by calling for Bathsheba to have sex with him while she was married to somebody else. Bathsheba did not call for David; as king, he inquired of who she was and sent his men to bring her to the palace. David also gave orders to deceitfully have Bathsheba's husband killed in battle to cover this sin.
6. Scripture does not tell of any attempt that David made to correct Amnon. It appears that Amnon was able to continue his business as if he had done no wrong.

Answer Key

7. According to the law, Amnon should have been killed for his actions. David did not carry out this consequence, even though as the father of the victim, he should have been the one to speak out on Tamar's behalf. Furthermore, as king, David certainly had the authority to make sure the law was carried out against Amnon.
8. After some time, Absalom rose up in his father's place to see that Amnon was killed for his actions.
9. David was very angry when he heard that Absalom had Amnon killed. Absalom fled and lived outside of the city. David refused to call for Absalom or allow him in his presence for a season.
10. God has given to each of us the gift of free will. This allows us to choose our own actions.
11. Joseph was mistreated and abused by his jealous half-brothers who sold him into slavery. When he was much older and wiser, Joseph concluded that God had allowed them to sell him into slavery for a greater purpose. Even though Joseph's half-brothers meant evil toward him, he understood that God meant it for good.
12. personal answer
13. Even the best earthly father is not as good as your heavenly Father.

Chapter Four

1. Forgiveness means freedom, liberty, pardon, to send away, let go, and release a debt that is owed to you.
2. Forgiveness says that everything is okay. If I have truly forgiven, then I will forget too. Forgiveness hurts the victim; the abuser does not deserve forgiveness. Revenge will give me peace.
3. personal answer
4. The Lord
5. God commands us to forgive.
6. personal answer
7. personal answer

8. Pray for the person(s) that you need to forgive. Forgiveness is more than a one-time event. Forgiveness is a choice.
9. personal answer
10. If you remain angry, you are giving a place to the devil, allowing him to stay and have access to your heart.

Chapter Five

1. Tamar probably felt like a loved princess that was destined for something great. She most likely felt special, beautiful, and important, especially when she wore her robe around the palace.
2. Since she remained desolate in her brother's house, it is likely that she felt rejected, alone, isolated, and without hope. She lost her future, royal position, dignity, self-worth, confidence, and ability to speak for herself.
3. Tamar wept bitterly, tore her special robe, and put ashes on her head.
4. The following scriptures are properly matched with what they tell us about grieving:
Judges 11:37- It is okay biblically to mourn for something that you will never know or experience.
I Samuel 16:1- God says stop mourning for something you cannot change.
Psalm 30:5- Weeping may endure for a night, but joy comes in the morning.
Ecclesiastes 3:1- For everything there is a season.
5. Grieving starts inwardly and may or may not be shown outwardly.
6. This is one explanation: Grieving involves setting aside an appointed time period to express emotions of sadness and loss over something that we lost.
7. Judges 11:34-40
8. personal answer
9. personal answer

10. personal answer

Chapter Seven

1. personal answer
2. personal answer
3. personal answer

About the Author

Misty Price is a sought-after Bible teacher who has spoken at churches, camps, retreats, and conferences for twenty-five years. She delivers a prophetic, timely word and is a testimony of God's power available to all of us to overcome the most challenging life circumstances, including bondages that have been passed down from generation to generation. She is an ordained minister with the Assemblies of God and holds a master of arts in theology and a master of science in education. Misty works alongside her husband, helping him pastor a thriving congregation in Carlsbad, New Mexico, and has two children.

End Notes

Merriam-Webster Online, "abuse," accessed August 20, 2019, https://www.merriam-webster.com/dictionary/abuse

Merriam-Webster Online, "desolate," accessed August 20, 2019, https://www.merriam-webster.com/dictionary/desolate

Strong's Exhaustive Concordance of the Bible- Biblehub online, "forgiveness," accessed August 21, 2019, https://biblehub.com/strongs/greek/859.htm

Strong's Exhaustive Concordance of the Bible- Biblehub online, "forgive," accessed August 21, 2019, https://biblehub.com/greek/863.htm

Cambridge Dictionary online, "subconscious," accessed August 24, 2019, https://dictionary.cambridge.org/us/dictionary/english/subconscious

To contact the author, order books, or get information about upcoming resources go to:

misty@carlsbadcalvary.com

CPSIA information can be obtained
at www.ICGtesting.com
Printed in the USA
FFHW021208181119
56067140-62059FF